The Risks of SOCIAL MEDIA

SOCIAL MEDIA **Shaming and Bullying**

Robert M. Henderson

San Diego, CA

About the Author

Robert M. Henderson has worked as an editor and copywriter for more than thirty years. He is the author of National Geographic's *World Regions: West Asia* and *The Spread of Hate and Extremism*. He currently lives in Vermont.

For more information, contact:
ReferencePoint Press, Inc.
PO Box 27779
San Diego, CA 92198
www.ReferencePointPress.com

Picture Credits:

Cover: Shutterstock.com
 5: fizkes/Shutterstock.com
11: pixelheadphoto/digitalskillet/Shutterstock.com
14: Aldo Murillo/iStock
16: Maury Aaseng
22: sirtravelalot/Shutterstock.com
25: JuliusKielaitis/Shutterstock.com
28: tommaso79/Shutterstock.com

30: Lopolo/Shutterstock.com
33: antoniodiaz/Shutterstock.com
38: Brent Eysler/Shutterstock.com
41: Jaguar PS/Shutterstock.com
45: Matheus Obst/Shutterstock.com
49: DGLimages/Shutterstock.com
50: fizkes/Shutterstock.com
54: Nuchylee/Shutterstock.com

LIBRARY OF CONGRESS CATALOGING-IN-PUBLICATION DATA

Names: Henderson, Robert M., author.
Title: Social media shaming and bullying / by Robert M. Henderson.
Description: San Diego, CA : ReferencePoint Press, Inc., 2021. | Series:
  The risks of social media | Includes bibliographical references and
  index.
Identifiers: LCCN 2020019628 (print) | LCCN 2020019629 (ebook) | ISBN
  9781682828571 (library binding) | ISBN 9781682828588 (ebook)
Subjects: LCSH: Cyberbullying--Juvenile literature. |
  Cyberbullying--Prevention--Juvenile literature. |
  Bullying--Prevention--Juvenile literature. | Shame--Juvenile literature.
Classification: LCC HV6773.15.C92 H46 2021 (print) | LCC HV6773.15.C92
  (ebook) | DDC 302.34/3--dc23
LC record available at https://lccn.loc.gov/2020019628
LC ebook record available at https://lccn.loc.gov/2020019629

Contents

A New Form of an Old Problem

On the evening of September 22, 2019, Tennessee high school student Channing Smith called people he knew in a panic. Screenshots of personal conversations he had had with another boy had been posted on Instagram and Snapchat. Until then, Channing had kept his sexuality private. "He was absolutely humiliated," said his older brother, who described the messages as "very explicit." He added, "There was no way he could have gone to school afterward."[1]

Later that evening, the sixteen-year-old posted a message to his Instagram followers. "I'm gonna get off social media for awhile. I really hate how I can't trust anyone because those I did were so fake. Bye."[2] At 4:00 a.m., Channing's father noticed that the light in the teen's bedroom was still on and went to investigate. Instead of finding Channing asleep, he discovered that his son had shot and killed himself. "My brother committed suicide because of the actions of 2 kids that he trusted that turned personal screen shot messages over to social media in a deliberate attempt to assassinate his character," wrote Channing's older brother on Facebook. He later added, "Nobody deserves to die as they are figuring their way through this complex journey called life."[3]

Channing's story affected many people throughout the country. Democratic presidential candidate Pete Buttigieg offered his condolences on social media, and country singer Billy Ray Cyrus attended a memorial service in Channing's hometown, where he sang "Amazing Grace" to an emotional audience. Later, Cyrus and members of the Smith family met with First Lady Melania Trump at the White House to share ideas about how to prevent online shaming and bullying.

"Nobody deserves to die as they are figuring their way through this complex journey called life."[3]

—Channing Smith's brother

Not Just a Teenage Problem

Shaming and bullying are not new, but the format has changed with the times. With the rise of the internet and social media, name-calling and rumor spreading have moved to platforms like Twitter, Facebook, and Instagram. Now, anyone with a smartphone can

Smartphones make it easy for anyone to anonymously post comments or images designed to shame or humiliate another person.

anonymously post comments, images, and posts designed to humiliate and shame another person.

Using social media to shame and bully also is not confined to tweens and teens; it is also happening in colleges, workplaces, and adult communities. American society places a high value on free speech, leading many people to believe they should be able to say whatever they want to whomever they want. This is not true, but it can be unclear where the line is drawn. And just because people *can* say things does not mean they *should*. It is not surprising that teens struggle with this problem because they often see the adults in their lives saying mean and nasty things to others without consequences.

To make matters even more complicated, some forms of online shaming are not necessarily "bad." Public shaming can be an effective way to hold people and organizations responsible for bad behavior. For example, public shaming can discourage predatory behavior in men and encourage greater respect for women. Or it might foster a boycott of a company that maintains discriminatory views against a segment of the country's population.

At the same time, online shaming can easily get out of hand. In today's era of smartphones and social media, it is easy to post an incriminating photo or video for everyone to see, but the ramifications for the shamed individual can last a long time. "People have long been called out and criticized publicly for breaching social norms," says Guy Aitchison, an Irish Research Council fellow at University College Dublin. "What's new today is that technology allows this to be immediately recorded and shared with millions of other unknown internet users. . . . A whole global audience is then invited to join in with ridicule and abuse and this often spills over into the target's personal life."[4]

Life-and-Death Consequences

People who have been publicly shamed, perhaps for posting some poorly considered joke on social media, can experience job loss, death threats, and social isolation. The shamed person often does not even get a chance to apologize, and those who participate in the mass shaming usually do not care.

Young people are especially vulnerable because they are still developing their personalities. Many teenage victims of shaming and bullying experience a variety of physical and mental health problems, including anxiety and depression, changes in sleep and eating patterns, increased feelings of loneliness and sadness, and a lack of interest in favorite activities. Bullying victims are also nearly two times more likely to attempt suicide than their nonbullied peers.

Many teens who have shamed or bullied others have told researchers they thought it was funny. But they often do not consider the powerful consequences of their actions. Bullies and their parents can face legal charges. And the damage they do to others can be lasting and permanent. At a vigil for her son, Channing Smith's mother told the crowd, "Just because you think it's cute or funny to make somebody embarrassed or humiliate them, think again. Because if somebody would have realized that, my son would not be dead."[5]

"Just because you think it's cute or funny to make somebody embarrassed or humiliate them, think again."[5]

—Channing Smith's mother

Chapter One

The Rise of Cyberbullying

Channing Smith's suicide has called attention to the growing problem of cyberbullying, which the National Crime Prevention Council defines as bullying "using the internet, cell phones, video game systems, or other technology to send or post text or images intended to hurt or embarrass another person."[6] Some cyberbullying crosses the line into unlawful or criminal behavior.

According to a 2018 report by the Pew Research Center, 95 percent of teens in the United States are online, 85 percent are social media users, and most of them access the internet through their smartphones. Because this technology has become such a big part of their lives, it should not be surprising that some teens have decided to use their phones to bully others. Being constantly connected means that teens are now susceptible to bullying around the clock. And because some adults are not aware of cyberbullying or how to respond to it properly, many bullies feel they can act with impunity.

The Pew Research Center reports that 59 percent of teens have experienced some form of cyberbullying, and 90 percent of them say it is a major problem for kids their age. Meanwhile, teachers report that cyberbullying is their top safety concern in the classroom, according to a 2019 Google survey.

A More Painful Form of Bullying

Mallory Grossman was a twelve-year-old from New Jersey who loved cheerleading and gymnastics. When she began middle school, a group of children started to torment her. They took photos of her without her knowledge and posted them online. "They called her horrible names, told her you have no friends and said, when are you going to kill yourself,"[7] her mother reported. Unfortunately, by the time Mallory's mother became fully aware of the cyberbullying, it was too late. On June 14, 2017, Mallory committed suicide.

Young people like Mallory who are victims of cyberbullying often experience more severe trauma than those who are bullied in person. Both kinds of bullying can be devastating, but there are several factors that can make cyberbullying seem more extreme to its victims.

The anonymous nature of the internet allows bullies to hide behind their computer screens without revealing themselves. Because they do not have to come face-to-face with their victims, bullies can act in especially malicious and menacing ways. Some bullies might not even grasp the tremendous harm they are causing because they cannot see the other person's reaction. For the victims, not knowing who is responsible for the bullying can add to their insecurity. "In real-life bullying, you know [who is] doing it," says fourteen-year-old Skye. On the internet, she says, "it could be someone you know, someone you don't know—you don't know what you know, and it's scary because it's really out of control at that point. Teachers tell you with bullying [to] just say 'Stop,' but in this case you can't, and you don't even know who to tell stop to."[8]

Hurtful text and images posted online can easily go viral. Instead of remaining a private matter between a small group of people, online bullying can reach a large audience very quickly. "Bullied children experience shame and humiliation," says bullying expert and author Mildred Peyton. "When they see others ridiculing them online they worry who else saw it, shared it—how far their image traveled." Some adults say the solution to online bullying is simple—the victims should turn off their phones. But this does not solve the problem. "Even if a child isn't online pictures of them can still be circulated by their peers," says Peyton, "and they are humiliated in school when they find out."[9]

Material posted on the internet is often permanent. This means that hurtful images and comments may be seen by colleges, employers, and others, now or in the future. In these cases, online shaming and bullying do not harm just the victim but can also negatively impact those participating in the bullying.

Finding No Escape

One of the most devastating effects of cyberbullying is the loss of the home as a safe space. Traditional bullying usually ends when victims enter the safety of their homes and are surrounded by family. But cyberbullying happens just as much in the home as anywhere else. "I go to school and get bullied. Go home and online and still get bullied. I can't ever escape it,"[10] says one fourteen-year-old boy.

Cyberbullying can be hard for parents and teachers to detect. A child can experience online bullying—or participate in bullying—without showing any outward signs. Many adults do not understand the technology well enough to recognize cyberbullying. And teens are often reluctant to tell their parents what is happening because they worry about being cut off from the internet. "Many parents do not understand how vital the Internet is to their social lives," say Jaana Juvonen, a professor of psychology at the University of California, Los Angeles. "Parents can take detrimental action with good intentions, such as trying to protect their children by not letting them use the Internet at all. That is not likely to help parent-teen relationships or the social lives of their children."[11]

Not only can cyberbullying seem more traumatic to its victims than traditional bullying, but there are also many more ways that kids can bully others using the internet. Most cyberbullying falls into one of five categories: harassment; impersonation; using photographs and videos; creating polls, websites, and blogs; and interactive gaming.

Harassment

The most common form of cyberbullying is harassment, which can include name-calling, spreading false rumors, stalking, and physical threats. According to the Pew Research Center, 42 percent of adolescents report being called offensive names. About a third (32 percent) of teens have been victims of false rumors that have been spread about them online. This occurs more frequently with girls (39 percent) than boys (26 percent). About one in five teens (21 percent) report having someone other than a parent constantly asking their whereabouts and whom they are with, while 16 percent say they have been the target of physical threats online.

In a 2019 survey, leading antibullying group Ditch the Label asked students who had been bullied in the previous twelve months why they thought they were bullied. More than half of the students (59 percent) said it was because of their physical appearance. Many of those same students also said it was about the way they dressed, indicating that how one looks is the most common reason for being victimized.

Teens are bullied for their weight or body shape, their hair and makeup, their height, their complexion—any part of how they look can be turned into a body flaw. The way people look is a large part of their identity. Comments about physical appearance and the way an individual dresses are not funny or trivial. They hurt very deeply.

According to Heather Widdows, a professor at the University of Birmingham in England and the founder of the social media campaign #EverydayLookism, "We need to take this form of bullying very seriously or the epidemic of body image anxiety can spiral out of control. Lookism is discrimination, and in a world where appearance increasingly matters, a particularly devastating form of discrimination. Appearance bullying is one of the most prevalent forms of bullying and one we should call a halt to."

Quoted in Ditch the Label, "The Annual Bullying Survey 2019." www.ditchthelabel.org.

Other forms of harassment include the pranks known as warning wars and text wars. Many social media sites feature a "warn button," which can be used to report someone who is behaving inappropriately. Teens will repeatedly click on these warn buttons as a way to get the victim kicked offline for a period. Text wars occur when teens send thousands of text messages to the victim's phone. This leaves a victim feeling overwhelmed by often hateful messages. The victim might also face a large phone bill (if texting is limited)—and, in turn, angry parents.

Impersonation

Impersonation is when the cyberbully pretends to be someone else online. For example, if a female classmate wants to bully another girl, she can create a fake social media account in a boy's name. The "boy" will then initiate an online relationship with the girl. Even though she has never met the boy in person, the victim might reveal personal information about herself. The classmate who is impersonating the boy can then share this information with others, who can use it to bully, shame, and harass the victim.

Bullies can also impersonate the victim. They might create an account and pose as the victim in the chat rooms of dating sites or hate groups. The bully may even reveal the victim's personal information, such as an email address, and encourage those in the chat rooms to contact the victim personally. Bullies can also steal the password to the victim's social media account and impersonate the victim by posting mean comments about his or her friends, thus angering and offending them.

Using Photographs and Videos

A particularly damaging form of cyberbullying is when someone takes a photo or video of the victim without his or her knowledge or consent. These unauthorized images are then uploaded for the world to see and discuss or criticize. Because they can be circulated endlessly on the internet, these images can be very hard to remove. Bullies can use photos and images in a variety of hurtful situations. Sometimes, people willingly take a sexually explicit photo or video of themselves and then share it with an intimate partner. When the relationship ends, the partner may post the photo or video online as a form of "revenge porn."

Many teens also report receiving unwanted sexually explicit images on their phones because the sender thinks it is funny or even enticing. Those who receive these images, though, might view the act as threatening. According to the Pew Research Center, girls are more likely than boys to report receiving explicit images (29 percent versus 20 percent). Older girls, ages fifteen to seventeen, are especially vulnerable to this type of bullying—35 percent of girls in this age group report having received unwanted explicit images, compared to 20 percent of the boys. Parents are particularly concerned about this kind of bullying. More than half (57 percent) report being worried about their children either getting or sending explicit images, according to a Pew Research Center survey of parents.

The photos and videos that are used to bully do not have to be sexual in nature. For example, Ashawnty Davis, a ten-year-old from Colorado, confronted her bully in the schoolyard one day. A fight broke out between them, and another student filmed the incident and uploaded it to the smartphone app Musical.ly, which is popular with elementary children. Ashawnty was devastated, her mother said: "My daughter came home two weeks later and hanged herself in the closet."[12]

Creating Polls, Websites, and Blogs

Another popular cyberbullying method is to create an online poll about the victim. Questions typically revolve around criticism of the person's appearance, weight, intelligence, or sexuality. Polls are easy to create and can attract the interest of many teens. Cyberbullies can also create websites or blogs for the sole purpose of bullying someone. These sites might feature unflattering photos of the victim, contain screenshots of cruel texts or comments, or expose personal information. "I've had at least 10 hate pages made about me," says fifteen-year-old Annie. "I know some were made in a row by the same person, but some were from different people. They say really nasty things about you, the most outrageous as possible."[13]

Interactive Gaming

Playing video games is one of the most popular activities among teens, with 72 percent saying they game online. Many play online with friends, classmates, and strangers. Players often use avatars to create fictional versions of themselves, which is part of the fun. But the anonymous nature of gaming can also lead to cyberbullying. Teens can gang up on a player by sending negative messages or excluding the player from the game.

Girls can experience more harsh forms of bullying while gaming than boys. The bullying they receive tends to be gendered, meaning other players will use sexually explicit language that is often demeaning and violent. For this reason, many girl gamers do not reveal their gender and play with their mics off.

Celebrities Also Get Cyberbullied

Celebrities are not immune from the cruelty of cyberbullies. In fact, many of the biggest stars in show business have been victims of cyberbullying, including Selena Gomez, Zayn Malik, and Lorde.

Selena Gomez was the fifth most-followed person on Instagram in 2020, but she does not always enjoy using the app because of the negative comments. "Imagine all the insecurities that you already feel about yourself and having someone write a paragraph pointing out every little thing, even if it's just physical," she says.

Zayn Malik suffered abuse from cyberbullies while in the band One Direction. Most of the bullying concerned his race. "Nasty things [were said] like I'm a terrorist, and this and that." What affected him the most was when the bullying reached members of his family. "When it starts to upset people I care about or I hear about it from my mum, then that's a problem."

Lorde has sold millions of albums, but in the early days of her career she experienced fierce cyberbullying concerning the way she looked. "The way I dress and carry myself, a lot of people find it strange or intimidating. . . . I'm not completely impervious to insult. I'm a human being."

Quoted in BBC Radio 1, "7 Stars Who Have Personal Experiences of Online Bullying." www.bbc.co.uk.

Where Does Cyberbullying Take Place?

A lot of cyberbullying takes place on social media platforms. According to Ditch the Label, one of the world's leading antibullying groups, 42 percent of teens report being bullied on Instagram, compared to 37 percent on Facebook and 31 percent on Snapchat. These results are not surprising. Facebook and Instagram (which is owned by Facebook) have struggled in recent years to control the tremendous amount of toxic content and misinformation found on their services.

Millions of teens visit Instagram regularly to check on their peers. According to a 2018 survey, 85 percent of teens said they used Instagram at least once a month. The site is perfectly designed to give users FOMO, or the "fear of missing out" on some

Social Media Sites Where Teens Report Cyberbullying

A leading antibullying group called Ditch the Label surveyed over ten thousand teenagers in the United Kingdom in 2017 to learn about their experiences with cyberbullying. According to the survey results, the social media platforms where teens most often experience cyberbullying are Instagram, Facebook, and Snapchat.

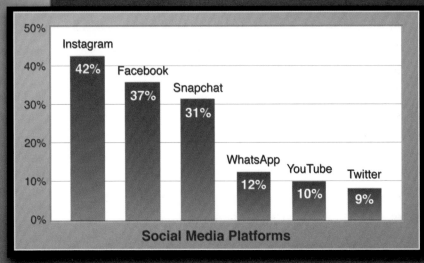

Where Are Young People Cyberbullied?

Source: "51 Critical Cyberbullying Statistics in 2020," Broadband Search, 2020. www.broadbandsearch.net.

news or event update. As one fourteen-year-old girl puts it, "Lots of bullying stems from jealousy, and Instagram is the ultimate jealousy platform. People are constantly posting pics of their cars, their bodies. Anything good in your life or at school goes on Insta, and that makes people jealous."[14]

The speed and size of Instagram means that cruel comments and humiliating images can go viral in a matter of hours. It is also easy to create anonymous profiles that can be used to bully other users. And the interactions that take place on Instagram are largely hidden from teachers and parents, many of whom do not understand the intricacies of the platform.

Recently, Instagram introduced features to help prevent bullying and make the platform a safer and more welcoming place. But many critics are skeptical. They charge the company with having made billions of dollars in profits while creating a culture of social media bullying. "Where were they five years ago?" questions Jim Steyer, the chief executive of Common Sense Media, a nonprofit watchdog group that champions increased protections on technology for children and teens. "This has been a huge issue for years, and most of these companies buried their heads in the sand until they were under pressure to do something about it."[15]

While social media platforms are taking a stronger stand against cyberbullying, questions remain about how effective their efforts are. For example, taking down content does not address the reasons why the bullying is happening in the first place. And victims who block or mute content may wonder what is being said about them behind their backs. Nevertheless, social media companies have an important role to play in reducing cyberbullying, but their efforts are only a part of the solution. Bullying is a broad societal issue that ultimately requires a response from everyone involved, including parents, teachers, school administrators, and the teens themselves.

Chapter Two

Using Social Media to Publicly Shame

Ryan Morgan is a white high school student from the Midwest who is growing up in a largely conservative town. In February 2019, the teen appeared on the cover of *Esquire* magazine. He was the subject of a story titled "An American Boy," which was part one of the magazine's Growing Up in America Today series.

Ryan's appearance on the cover of *Esquire* sparked outrage online. One Twitter user wrote, "*Esquire* dropping this ode to white male privilege that no one asked for . . . during Black History month is just . . . ugh." [16] Another said, "I cannot think of a topic less worthy of exploration than this."[17] While many social media users criticized the magazine for doing the story, others attacked Ryan himself. Some wanted to punch him. Others suggested sending him hate mail. A few people on Twitter just swore at him.

But others were disturbed that a teenager should be on the receiving end of such public venom. After all, one of the points of the magazine story was that young people like Ryan are struggling to form their thoughts and opinions about the complexities of the world in which they live. "The story is not offensive and Morgan seems like . . . a kid. Watching [him] get flamed on Twitter is a bummer,"[18] wrote one columnist.

What happened to Ryan Morgan is an example of online shaming. This kind of shaming has a lot in common with cyberbullying, but there is a difference—people who publicly shame often believe they are righting a wrong. According to WhatIs.com, a leading resource for information technology, the definition of online shaming is "the use of social media, blogs and other online communication channels to attack a target individual or organization. The purpose of the attack is often to publicly embarrass the target, often as retribution for some behavior."[19]

The difference between cyberbullying and online shaming is that cyberbullying is universally condemned as a bad thing, but online shaming may have value if it calls out bad behavior. But the consequences of online shaming can be just as severe and long-lasting as the consequences of cyberbullying. People who are publicly shamed can suffer from anxiety, depression, and suicidal thoughts, just like those who are cyberbullied. And public shaming is not temporary—the internet never forgets. In an opinion piece that appeared in *The New York Times* entitled *"Esquire's* Cover Boy and Our Culture of Shame," author Robyn Kanner writes, "Digital shaming is arguably the only punishment that does not have a statute of limitations. Do we really want to live in a culture like this? Where no one has the room to grow or change or become a new version of him or herself?"[20]

> "Digital shaming is arguably the only punishment that does not have a statute of limitations."[20]
>
> —Robyn Kanner, a writer and designer

Public Shaming Makes a Comeback

Shaming is one of the oldest forms of punishment and was often used in early America. The Puritans punished people by placing them in wooden stocks in the village square or by publicly whipping them. Children who did poorly in school or misbehaved were sometimes forced to wear a dunce cap and sit on a stool in the corner.

Things began to change during the late eighteenth century. Many public leaders began to view public shaming as cruel and warned that well-meaning citizens, when gathered in a crowd, often became a mob that took punishment too far. Founding Father Benjamin Rush wrote in 1787 that public shaming "is universally acknowledged to be a worse punishment than death."[21] In 1791, the Eighth Amendment to the US Constitution was adopted, which formally banned "cruel and unusual punishment." As a result, the public stockade was abolished by law, and schools started to phase out humiliating punishments like the dunce cap. Parents were told to stop shaming their children because it might damage their confidence. In fact, the first use of the popular word *self-esteem* can be traced back to 1856.

Of course, public shaming never really went away. But for a long time, it was limited to subjects that newspaper editors and television producers chose to cover. For example, in the 1990s, the extramarital affair between President Bill Clinton and twenty-two-year-old White House intern Monica Lewinsky dominated the media. The public shaming and bullying that Lewinsky experienced severely damaged her reputation and came close to ruining her life.

Now, with the emergence of the internet and social media, public shaming has moved from newspapers and television to platforms like Facebook and Twitter. The power to shame others is no longer confined to media leaders like editors and producers. Now anyone can do it, and it is as simple as opening an app. What is more, people can engage in shaming on the internet without revealing themselves. This has had a profound effect on the power of shaming and its resurgence.

Today, public shaming is practically a blood sport. Social media users not only shame others for mistakes they made today but also for mistakes they made years ago. For example, immediately after comedian Trevor Noah was named as the new host of *The Daily Show*, people on Twitter attacked him over some Tweets he had made in the past. "It's so corrosive to create that kind of society," says Jon Ronson, the author of *So You've Been*

In August 2017, white supremacists held a large protest rally in Charlottesville, Virginia, that attracted national attention. Soon photos of the protesters began to appear on a Twitter account called Yes, You're Racist. This account sought to shame the protesters by exposing their identities online. As a result, some of the protesters were fired from their jobs. One was disowned by his family. Another was a case of mistaken identity, which nevertheless resulted in death threats and accusations of racism.

The act of revealing identifying information about someone online is known as doxing, which is short for "dropping docs." In the 1990s, doxing was a revenge tactic among hackers that involved stealing someone's personal information and publishing it online. Today, doxing is most associated with shaming neo-Nazis and other extremists.

For many, identifying people participating in a white supremacist rally is a just punishment for being openly hateful. But doxing can also expose people to widespread harassment and even physical danger. "Doxing is a sloppy form of justice that often hurts many beyond the intended target," says Jared Colton, who teaches about ethics and technology at Utah State University. "It punishes their families and even people who look like them or have similar names."

Quoted in Emma Grey Ellis, "Whatever Your Side, Doxing Is a Perilous Form of Justice," *Wired*, August 17, 2017. www.wired.com.

Publicly Shamed. "This desire we have to be like amateur detectives, (looking for) clues into people's inherent evil by finding the worst tweet they ever wrote, is not only wrong; it's damaging."[22]

Rushing to Judgment

Information travels like lightning on social media, and users react with equal speed. The format of platforms like Twitter and Facebook encourage people to share "hot takes," or quick reactions, rather than carefully considered responses. And these hot takes can spread around the world very quickly, sometimes only hours after a controversial incident.

In 2013, public relations executive Justine Sacco was flying from New York to South Africa to visit family. She began tweeting little jokes, including one that said, "Going to Africa. Hope I don't get AIDS. Just kidding. I'm white!"[23] Sacco only had 170 followers, but someone from a popular news and gossip website saw the tweet and retweeted it to his followers, who numbered in the thousands. Within hours, it became Twitter's top worldwide trend.

Tens of thousands of angry tweets had responded to Sacco's tweet, most along the lines of "How did @JustineSacco get a PR job?! Her level of racist ignorance belongs on Fox News. #AIDS can affect anyone!"[24] Even her employer responded to the tweet: "This is an outrageous, offensive comment. Employee in question currently unreachable on an intl flight."[25] Another person tweeted gleefully, "We are about to watch this @JustineSacco . . . get fired. In REAL time. Before she even KNOWS she's getting fired."[26] As Sacco slept on her eleven-hour flight, a hashtag began to trend worldwide: #HasJustineLandedYet. One Twitter user even went to the airport in South Africa to tweet about her arrival and take her photograph.

Usually, there is no preexisting relationship between the person being shamed and the people doing the shaming.

Justine Sacco's story is a vivid illustration of the incredible power of the internet to dissemi-

nate information very quickly to a huge number of people. Most social media users simply do not grasp the vast power of the medium. They unthinkingly post comments and believe they are whispering to a small group of followers. But the reality is they are speaking through a megaphone whose volume can be turned up so the whole world can hear.

When it comes to online shaming, the vast power of the internet often means the punishment will be much greater than the crime warrants. This is especially true when the shaming goes viral and affects the offender's personal life—potentially forever. Father James Martin, a priest and the editor of *America* magazine, says that what begins as disapproval ends up "as a complete shaming of the person. There's a real cruelty that comes with this mob mentality," he says. "I sometimes compare it to bullies in a schoolyard all ganging up on person who, for one second, said the wrong thing."[27]

Another major problem with online public shaming is that it often lacks context. There is usually no preexisting relationship between the people doing the shaming and the person being shamed. The result is that, sometimes, the shaming is triggered by a misunderstanding. Sacco claimed her tweet was a joke, mimicking—and mocking—what an actual racist person would say. But the thousands of people who shamed her on Twitter did not know her personally. They simply took her tweet at face value.

> "There's a real cruelty that comes with this mob mentality."[27]
>
> —Father James Martin, the editor of *America* magazine

In an ironic twist, reporter Sam Biddle, the man who first retweeted Sacco's offensive tweet, later found himself on the wrong end of Twitter's outrage machine. He was publicly shamed on Twitter for tweeting a joke of his own that said, "Bring Back Bullying." Perhaps humbled to find himself in a situation similar to Sacco's, he published a public apology to her, saying, "Twitter is a fast machine that almost begs for misunderstanding and misconstrual—deliberate misreading is its lubricant. The same flatness of affect that can make it such a weird and funny place

Individuals are not the only ones who shame others online—governments can do it too, particularly in China, where public shaming is a common tactic. For example, in Chinese theaters, ushers use laser pointers to shame members of the audience who use their phones during shows.

But in January 2020 the government went too far when it used facial recognition software to target a relatively common practice in China—wearing pajamas in public. To try to prevent people from doing this, the government posted photos online of several people wearing pajamas in public, along with their names, government identification, and where their "uncivilized behavior" had occurred.

Some critics were outraged that the government chose to post personal information so publicly. Others simply wondered what was so wrong with wearing pajamas outside. Fashion blogger Hung Huang says the government should not be interfering in the fashion choices of Chinese citizens. "In China, when these things happen, it is when very high technology gets into the hands of very low-level bureaucrats, and by low level I mean low level of intelligence," Hung says. "This should be an alarm for all Chinese tech developers and Chinese government policymakers."

Quoted in Amy Qin, "Chinese City Uses Facial Recognition to Shame Pajama Wearers," *New York Times*, January 21, 2020. www.nytimes.com.

also makes it a tricky and dangerous one. Jokes are complicated, context is hard. Rage is easy."[28]

How Computer Algorithms Promote Outrage

Social media companies like Facebook, Twitter, and YouTube use computer algorithms that are designed to "nudge" users into viewing content that will keep them engaged. The longer a user stays on the platform, the more money the company makes. These companies are fully aware that users are especially drawn to material that is extreme and outrageous, so social media platforms tend to favor that kind of provocative content. Former YouTube engineer Guillaume Chaslot reported that the algorithms he worked on heavily promoted divisive issues "because divisiveness is effi-

"Jokes are complicated, context is hard. Rage is easy."[28]

—Sam Biddle, a reporter for The Intercept

cient for watch time, and watch time leads to ads."[29] This is why strongly worded, emotional posts—such as those shaming individuals—get so much attention. When users engage with this kind of content by clicking or sharing, they give a positive signal to the algorithm, which then boosts that content even more. This is how some material—such as Sacco's tweet—goes viral.

These "recommendation" algorithms have a tremendous impact on how we consume information today. According to Chaslot, YouTube users spend 700 million hours each day watching videos recommended by the algorithm. Meanwhile, the algorithm for Facebook's news feed is responsible for around 950 million hours of viewing time per day. This algorithmic nudging creates what is called an echo chamber effect, whereby users are presented with information and opinions that tend to agree with their existing beliefs. In 2019, researchers at Google examined the impact of recommendation systems, such as those used by YouTube and other platforms. It was clear, they concluded, that "feedback loops in recommendation systems can give rise to 'echo chambers' and 'filter bubbles,' which can narrow a user's content exposure and ultimately shift their worldview."[30]

Social media platforms such as YouTube tend to favor content that is provocative in order to attract and engage viewers.

This problem is worsened by the fact that more people are now turning to social media as their primary source of news. According to a 2019 Pew Research Center report, more than half (55 percent) of American adults receive their news "often" or "sometimes" from social media. Almost a third of Americans (28 percent) said they "often" get their news from social media—a 20 percent increase from 2018. The report concluded that "social media is now a part of the news diet of an increasingly large share of the U.S. population."[31]

The problem, however, is that social media platforms are not designed to inform people in an objective, nonbiased manner. Instead, it is just the opposite. They are designed to engage the user, and what engages the user the most is sensationalist, divisive content that often reinforces that individual's social, political, or cultural beliefs. Why does a story about a white, conservative teenager on the cover of *Esquire* go viral on Twitter? Because the platform's algorithm decided that certain users—most likely urban, progressive liberals—would be engaged, or more accurately, outraged by that piece of content. The result was a massive rush of condemnation for both the magazine and the subject of its cover story, seventeen-year-old Ryan Morgan.

Some Twitter users were quick to point out the dynamics of this ideological piling on. One wrote, "Why your ideological echo chamber isn't just bad for you, it's also bad for your kids. Kudos to @esquire for having the courage to stand up to the social media/identity politics mob."[32] Another user noted, "The reactions to this article are exactly what you'd expect in 2019. *Esquire* writes a plain vanilla bio on an incredibly average white kid from middle America and there's still outrage and a sense of disdain for him and anyone like him."[33] Even though comments like these might seem like they are correcting an overreaction, they are still feeding the controversy, which is exactly what social media companies want. Endless controversy means more clicks, shares—and revenue—and the vicious cycle of never-ending outrage continues.

Chapter Three

The Trauma of Being Bullied or Publicly Shamed

Freelance journalist Caitlin White was eating in a restaurant when a tweet she had posted earlier that day suddenly became the target of heated criticism. While she was having dinner with her siblings, her phone alerted her that an online community of peers was ridiculing her for her supposed insensitivity. According to White, her tweet had compared "the rhetoric of a blame-shifting police statement about the fatal shooting of yet another young, unarmed black man to the victim-blaming rhetoric of domestic abusers." Unable to enjoy her food, she sat glued to her phone. "I was frozen, stung," she explains, "the poison pooled and spread into my evening. Physical chills coursed through my body, my appetite disappeared. It was excruciating."[34]

Victims of online shaming or bullying can experience a wide range of emotions, from mild embarrassment to extreme fear. But nobody likes to be attacked or criticized by their peers. And when those criticizers are online, they can be especially cruel because they do not have to confront their victims face-to-face. Even when the abuse stops, many victims continue to live in fear, waiting for the next incident to occur. One professional writer confided that he was harassed for weeks online after publishing an unpopular opinion. The experience was so unpleasant that, years later, he still discusses it with his therapist. "I basically spent 48 hours refreshing Twitter every three minutes, worried someone new was going to pile on," he says. "It was to the point where I didn't sleep much, and I couldn't think of anything else. . . . I don't know if I've ever gotten over that existential fear."[35]

The importance of people's online, or digital, selves continues to grow as the internet becomes increasingly integrated into their personal, academic, and professional lives. It is becoming less and less possible to simply live offline. The internet has become a workplace, a town hall, and an increasingly indispensable way to connect with others. Some media scholars argue that the separation between people's physical and digital selves is dramatically shrinking. "People are enmeshing their physical and digital selves to the point where the distinction is becoming increasingly

Many victims of online shaming and bullying continue to live in fear, waiting for the next incident to occur.

irrelevant,"[36] writes social media theorist Nathan Jurgenson. This means that the hurt and trauma a person may experience online is just as devastating as any other kind of trauma, and in some ways, even more so.

Toxic Emotions

"Shame is a soul eating emotion,"[37] wrote Swiss psychoanalyst Carl Gustav Jung. And anyone who has been bullied or shamed, online or off, knows exactly what he means. In recent decades, psychology research has found that feelings of shame can profoundly demoralize and damage people. It is a feeling that is much worse than guilt because guilt focuses on a person's actions, but shame focuses on a person's character and identity. "Guilt is 'I made a mistake.' Shame is 'I am a mistake,'"[38] says Vicki Underland-Rosow, the author of *Shame, Spiritual Suicide*.

Feeling shame is incredibly difficult for adults to bear, but it is even harder for young people, who have not yet developed the coping mechanisms to deal with such a powerfully negative emotion. That is why teens can feel totally overwhelmed by cyberbullying, and they often report being paralyzed by fear, loneliness, and despair. Many teens who

are bullied simply cannot see a way out, and this hopelessness can lead to depression and self-harm. "Children can't solve bullying themselves," says Laura Crothers, a psychology professor at Duquesne University. "That's probably one of the biggest mistakes that adults make, is thinking that kids can figure it out themselves or they'll get through it on their own. We haven't seen that to be the case in the literature."[39]

Cyberbullies often attack where their targets are the most vulnerable. The pain inflicted upon an already weak spot causes victims to quickly lose their sense of worth and value. Soon their self-confidence and self-esteem are replaced by shame and hu-miliation. Many victims start to believe that they deserve all the bad things that are happening to them. Some try to fix the vulnerable part of themselves in the hope the bullying will stop. One thirteen-year-old girl writes, "People made fun of how I looked, the amount of food I ate. . . . At first I didn't really think of it but then it started ringing in my head that I didn't look like the popular girls and I thought that maybe if I was skinny they would be my friends. This later led me into developing an eating disorder and I also started to self-harm."[40]

Shame can also lead to feelings of anger, irritability, and hos-tility. Sometimes people who feel shame will lash out, but most victims internalize it, which leads to depression. Unable to cope with these negative feelings, many teenage victims of cyberbul-lying eventually reach a point where the internalized anger is so powerful that it needs to be released in some way. But instead of resorting to violence against others, victims of cyberbullying most

Teenage victims of cyberbullying often turn their anger on themselves, leading to self-harm and attempts at suicide.

Self-Abuse Online: A Disturbing New Trend

One night in 2016, a fifteen-year-old from Texas named Natalie Natividad took her own life after enduring months of cyberbullying. Her suicide prompted an investigation. "We just want some justice," said Natalie's sister shortly after the death. "Whoever is bullying, I hope that they stop." But no bullies were ever found. The investigation revealed that Natalie had secretly cyberbullied herself. Researchers call this digital self-harm, and it is becoming more common. A 2019 study showed that nearly 9 percent of American teens have done this to themselves, up from 6 percent in 2016.

But why would anyone do such a thing? Ana, now twenty years old, says that when she was fourteen, she anonymously posted abusive messages to herself in the hopes that people would defend her. This type of behavior is similar to "sadfishing," which is when someone posts exaggerated accounts of their emotional state in order to receive attention and sympathy from others.

The phenomenon of digital self-harm is still not well understood. Researchers have been mystified by its recent increase. "People are uniformly shocked to learn that this problem exists," says Justin Patchin, a professor of criminal justice at the University of Wisconsin–Eau Claire.

Quoted in *The Economist*, "Why More Young Americans Are Cyber-Bullying Themselves," January 11, 2020. www.economist.com.

often direct the violence onto themselves, leading to self-harm and attempts at suicide.

When cyberbullying is persistent and severe enough, it can lead to post-traumatic stress disorder (PTSD) when the victims get older. PTSD is a mental health condition that is caused by experiencing or witnessing a terrible event. Symptoms may include severe anxiety, nightmares, and unwanted memories of the event. According to a 2020 study published in the *Journal of Clinical Psychiatry*, cyberbullying was shown to directly amplify symptoms of PTSD in young people. "Being bullied is not a harmless rite of passage or an inevitable part of growing up," says Dieter Wolke, a psychology professor at the University of Warwick in England. "It has serious long-term consequences."[41]

The Shocking Rise in Teen Suicides

In October 2019, the Centers for Disease Control and Prevention published a report that startled health professionals. The suicide rate among young people was fairly steady from 2000 to 2007 but then from 2007 to 2017 it increased by 56 percent. With that change, suicide became the second-leading cause of death for people ages ten to twenty-four. "We're at a point now where this issue really can't be ignored,"[42] says John P. Ackerman, a clinical psychologist and the coordinator of suicide prevention at Nationwide Children's Hospital in Columbus, Ohio.

Perhaps coincidentally, the year that suicide rates started rising dramatically among young people—2007—also happened to be the same year that the iPhone was introduced. Because of the smartphone, social media platforms like YouTube, Facebook, and Twitter exploded in popularity. In 2008, Facebook had around 100 million users. By 2018, that number had grown to over 2 billion.

This direct correlation between the rise of social media and the rise of teen suicide rates has caught the attention of experts everywhere. However, it is important to remember that correlation is not the same as causation. Many health professionals are wary of only blaming smartphones and social media for the rise in suicide rates among young people. Ultimately, no one can say with certainty why suicide has become such a crisis among the young. Nevertheless, most experts agree that social media has played a role, especially for young people who are already at risk for anxiety and depression. "Developmentally, these ages have always been difficult, but that's been taken to the next level by smartphones, social media and the constant pressure to be online," says Jean M. Twenge, a research psychologist at San Diego State University and the author of *iGen*. "It's now the norm to sit home Saturday night on Instagram. Who's popular and who's not is now quantifiable by how many people are following you. Kids are spending as much as eight hours a day on social media, where there's a lot of negativity, competition and jockeying for status."[43]

Teens themselves are somewhat conflicted about the role that social media plays in their lives. According to a 2018 Pew Research Center report, whereas most teens believe social media has played a positive role in their lives, others feel it has had a negative impact. Nearly half (45 percent) of teens report feeling overwhelmed by all the drama surrounding social media, and roughly 40 percent admit to feeling pressured to only post things that make them look good. And over a quarter (26 percent) of all young people say that social media makes them feel unhappy. "After hours of scrolling through Instagram feeds, I just feel worse about myself because I feel left out,"[44] says seventeen-year-old Caitlin Hearty.

Many health experts firmly believe that the rise in youth suicide is directly related to cyberbullying. One 2018 study showed that people under the age of twenty-five who were cyberbullied were twice as likely to self-harm or commit suicide. Regarding gender, the rise in suicide rates among young people is more pronounced among girls, perhaps because girls are more likely

Girls are more likely than boys to experience cyberbullying, and social media makes this style of aggression easier to employ.

to experience cyberbullying than boys. Boys tend to bully other kids physically, but girls prefer to target a victim's social status or relationships. Social media allows girls to employ the style of aggression they favor. "The twin rise of the smartphone and social media has caused an earthquake of a magnitude we've not seen in a very long time, if ever," says Twenge. "There is compelling evidence that the devices we've placed in young people's hands are having profound effects on their lives—and making them seriously unhappy."[45]

The Internet Never Forgets

Sue Scheff was one of the first people ever to feel the wrath of an online mob. It has been many years since she went through her harrowing experience, yet she still feels scarred by it. Her ordeal began in 2003 when she was running a parent advocacy group that helped troubled teens. A disgruntled client started posting nasty things online, calling Scheff a con artist and a crook who abused kids and exploited families.

As a result, Scheff was viciously attacked online by an angry mob of people. She received many hateful comments and even death threats. Eventually, Scheff won a defamation lawsuit against the client, but the victory felt hollow. "When the verdict was read, I had that moment of bliss," she says. "But then I quickly remembered, the internet never forgets. . . . There's no delete button online. Just when you think you're doing better, something can pop up and trigger your emotions. It is truly like PTSD. It isn't something you just move on from."[46]

Scheff is not alone. According to a 2017 Pew Research Center report, about 40 percent of Americans have been harassed online, and most (62 percent) believe it is a significant problem. Nearly one in five Americans (18 percent) have experienced especially severe forms of harassment, such as sexual harassment, stalking, physical threats, and long-term harassment. These online encounters can have profound and long-lasting consequences, ranging from mental and emotional distress to reputational damage to fear for one's personal safety.

In a 2019 survey by Ditch the Label, 34 percent of those who experienced bullying said the impact was moderate to extreme. Interestingly, 31 percent reported that being bullied had "no impact" on their lives. But is it really possible that something as painful as bullying could have absolutely no consequences on a person?

Being bullied is a traumatic experience, and sometimes people going through a traumatic experience simply repress their feelings and disassociate from what is going on. According to psychotherapist Rebecca Barrie, "Disassociating protects us from feeling too much and allows us to cope, to a point where we trick ourselves into believing that we are fine and the bullying is having no effect on us."

Although disassociating may work in the short term, the bad feelings that have been ignored tend to come back later and cause problems. For example, someone who was bullied at school might come across someone later in life who reminds them of that bully. This can act as a trigger, releasing the bad memories, which can cause anxiety. "Very often I see people who are suffering with panic attacks and don't understand why," says Barrie. "With a little digging, we can usually find the cause."

Quoted in Ditch the Label, "The Annual Bullying Survey 2018." www.ditchthelabel.org.

Justine Sacco is all too familiar with these consequences. After she lost her job for her tweet that went viral while she slept on a plane headed to South Africa, Sacco refused to talk to anyone for a long time. Eventually, she agreed to speak to a reporter from *The New York Times* because she felt it was necessary to show how crazy and difficult her experience had been, and how her punishment did not fit the crime. "I cried out my body weight in the first 24 hours," she recalled. "It was incredibly traumatic. You don't sleep. You wake up in the middle of the night forgetting where you are. . . . All of a sudden you don't know what you're supposed to do. If I don't start making steps to reclaim my identity and remind myself of who I am on a daily basis, then I might lose myself." She also mentioned one of the hidden costs of her ordeal. "I'm single; so it's not like I can date, because we Google everyone we might date," she said. "That's been taken away from me too."[47]

In order to remove their names from search engines like Google, people who have experienced online shaming sometimes hire companies that specialize in reputation management. These digital image rehabilitation firms cannot remove the incriminating stories from the search engines, but they try to add new positive stories about their clients that will push the negative stories to the second page of Google, where hardly anyone will see them. One of these companies is called ReputationDefender. "We hear everything under the sun," says Rich Matta, the company's chief executive officer (CEO). "'I can't get a job,' 'I'm just embarrassed by it,' 'I want to be remembered differently,' 'I don't want my kids to suffer from this,' sometimes even, 'I'm worried this is keeping me from getting a date.' There are so many different ways that online shaming can destroy people's lives and livelihoods."[48]

> "There are so many different ways that online shaming can destroy people's lives and livelihoods."[48]
>
> —Rich Matta, the CEO of ReputationDefender

Restoring a person's reputation on Google is easier said than done. Often, when people see an unfavorable or embarrassing search result, they click on it. This reinforces Google's conclusion that the result is important and relevant. Ultimately, the internet does not show mercy for people who make a mistake online, even if they are completely innocent. All it takes is one false move—and complete strangers can ruin your life.

Chapter Four

Calling Out Bad Behavior

On May 15, 2018, a video was posted on Facebook showing a very angry white man yelling at the manager of a New York eatery, complaining, "Your staff is speaking Spanish to customers when they should be speaking English. . . . This is America." One employee told the man his coworkers were simply talking with other customers. That did not satisfy the man, who pointed at those he heard speaking Spanish. "My guess is, they're not documented, so my next call is to ICE [US Immigration and Customs Enforcement] to have each one of [them] kicked out of my country," he said. "They have the balls to come here and live off of my money I pay for their welfare, I pay for their ability to be here. The least they could do, the least they could do is speak English."[49] The posted video quickly went viral, attracting over 5 million views during the first two days it appeared on Facebook.

The name of the man in the video is Aaron Schlossberg, and he is a Manhattan lawyer. A week after the incident, Schlossberg issued an apology, saying he is not a racist and was deeply sorry for his actions. However, it was discovered that Schlossberg had engaged in racist behavior

on at least four separate occasions during a two-year period. In 2009, for instance, he was arrested for disorderly conduct at a Philadelphia Phillies baseball game, where he disturbed other fans and threatened security officers.

Schlossberg quickly became the target of a massive public shaming campaign—both on- and offline. Customer ratings for his law practice on Yelp plummeted, his landlord terminated the lease for his offices, and reporters constantly hounded him seeking comment. There was even a protest outside his apartment building featuring a mariachi band and dancing. Most people applauded this public shaming. In an article titled "The Social Shaming of Racists Is Working," author Laila Lalami writes, "The ubiquitous presence of smartphones with cameras has helped to document such incidents, and social media have brought them to national attention. That's a useful development. . . . Maybe, just maybe, racists will think twice before making frivolous reports or issuing threats."[50]

The Benefits of Public Shaming

Shame has developed a bad reputation recently. Because shame is the favorite tool of bullies, most who use it intend to destroy the confidence and self-worth of their victims. But according to many historians, sociologists, and psychologists, shame has actually been a force for good for much of human history.

Studies in the field of evolutionary science show that shame developed because it helped encourage social cohesion. Long ago, when people lived in small tribes, human survival depended on everyone cooperating with each other. Individuals who broke the rules were shunned and shamed. This painful experience motivated people to work together, strengthening the tribe. Daniel Sznycer, the lead researcher in one study, explains, "The function of pain is to prevent us from damaging our own tissue. The function of shame is to prevent us from damaging our social relationships, or to motivate us to repair them."[51]

Today, the attractions of shaming are easy to see. America's legal system is limited in what it can do to punish individuals who break moral codes. Public shaming allows the public to avoid the messy business of law and policy. Instead, social norms can be enforced quickly and forcefully by public opinion. If the First Amendment protects racist speech, for example, critics can still shame people who make racist comments. Eric Posner, a professor at the University of Chicago Law School, says the appeal of public shaming is that it "seems like a democratic, cost-effective, and fluid device for combating environmental degradation, racism, and homophobia—for creating a virtuous society."[52]

> "The function of shame is to prevent us from damaging our social relationships, or to motivate us to repair them."[51]
>
> —Daniel Sznycer, an evolutionary biologist

Although many people are uncomfortable with the idea of "mob rule" dispensing justice, when it comes to exceptional cases like Aaron Schlossberg's rant, most people seem to agree with the virtue of shaming. After all, Schlossberg did not face legal repercussions for his racist comments. He is still practicing law today, even though many do not believe he is fit to do so. And while his speech is protected, that right does not protect him from the social consequences of his words, which might include harassment and ostracism.

While not always easy to define, Black Twitter is a virtual community featuring an array of black voices discussing issues that directly affect their community. "To me, Black Twitter is essentially an extension of my black urban experience," says writer Michael Arceneaux. "It's a bunch of people like me. Black people in major cities and its basically six degrees of separation. I might not know you, but I might have a friend of a friend of a friend who does."

During the 2010s, Black Twitter became a social media phenomenon that changed the national conversation about race and other topics. "As the saying goes, if society doesn't handle it, then Black Twitter will step in to handle it," says Mia Moody-Ramirez, a professor of journalism at Baylor University. On a lighter note, Black Twitter users also discuss movies, music, and television from the black perspective.

Many believe the influence and visibility of Black Twitter will continue through the 2020s. "As much as people complain about Twitter, it has a mindshare wildly out of proportion with its user base," says Georgia Tech professor André Brock. "I don't see a service that offers that same level of access, distribution and open conversation on the horizon."

Quoted in Soraya Nadia McDonald, "Black Twitter: A Virtual Community Ready to Hashtag Out a Response to Cultural Issues," *Washington Post,* January 20, 2014. www.washingtonpost.com.

Quoted in Gabrielle White, "What Is Black Twitter and How Is It Changing the National Conversation? Baylor Expert Explains," Baylor University, February 19, 2019. www.baylor.edu.

Quoted in André Wheeler, "Ten Years of Black Twitter: A Merciless Watchdog for Problematic Behavior," *The Guardian* (Manchester, UK), December 23, 2019. www.theguardian.com.

Many argue that if the law will not punish Schlossberg, society and public opinion should. "There is no indication that Schlossberg has misled a court, mishandled funds, or deceived a client," writes Mark Joseph Stern, who covers courts and law for Slate. "Until evidence of such malpractice emerges, no organ of the state has power to strip him of his law license. It's up to the rest of us to ensure that his career goes down the tubes where it belongs."[53]

Online Shaming as Political Activism

In 2018, popular comedian Kevin Hart was invited to host the 2019 Oscars. Shortly after he accepted, homophobic tweets of his from 2009 to 2011 surfaced and started circulating around the internet. Soon Hart found himself the target of an online shaming campaign. Insisting he was a changed man, Hart refused to apologize but stepped down from hosting the Oscars. Some people thought it was unfair to dig up Hart's old tweets, but others asserted that shaming was a fair and just way to expose homophobia and the damage it does to the LGBTQ community. "Forgive me if I care less about the comedian who made his own bed versus the people affected by the anti-queer climate he helped create,"[54] wrote *Esquire*'s Michael Arceneaux.

As we enter the 2020s, influential individuals like Hart can no longer avoid public scrutiny. Over the past few years, movements like Black Lives Matter and #MeToo have gained momentum through social media, especially Twitter. Sometimes this online activism is dismissively called cancel culture, but others argue that social media simply gives a voice to previously marginalized

After comedian Kevin Hart was invited to host the 2019 Oscars, homophobic tweets that he had posted years earlier came to light. The public shaming campaign that followed led him to step down from hosting the Oscars.

In October 2019, Barack Obama weighed in on the controversy surrounding online shaming and so-called cancel culture. "I get a sense among certain young people on social media that the way of making change is to be as judgmental as possible about other people," the former president said in an interview. "If I tweet or hashtag about how you didn't do something right or used the wrong verb, then I can sit back and feel pretty good about myself because 'Man did you see how woke I was? I called you out!'" He continued, "That's not activism. That's not bringing about change."

Obama's comments were met with approval by people on both sides of the political spectrum. Clips of the interview were shared and viewed millions of times on social media.

But not everyone agreed with Obama. "What people of Obama's generation don't understand is that we're not bullies going after people with 'different opinions' for sport," wrote Ernest Owens in the *New York Times*. "Rather, we're trying to push back against the bullies. . . . We have a tool that has helped democratize public debates about these issues. . . . It's called social media. And we're going to keep using it."

Quoted in BBC News, "Barack Obama Challenges 'Woke' Culture," October 30, 2019. www.bbc.com.

Ernest Owens, "Obama's Very Boomer View of 'Cancel Culture,'" *New York Times*, November 1, 2019. www.nytimes.com.

people. Shame, they say, can be harnessed for good, compelling people and organizations to adhere to society's social and moral norms.

One of the most powerful examples of how public shaming has had a positive effect is the #MeToo movement. By encouraging women to speak out, the movement has exposed and shamed many prominent men who abused their power to sexually exploit women. The hope is that this will reduce predatory behavior in men and promote greater respect for women. As journalist Emily J. Yoffe writes, "#MeToo is a necessary and important corrective to some horrifying, copiously documented, and criminal-level behavior, and also to the kind of persistent harassment that still characterizes too many workplaces."[55]

Not everyone agrees that online shaming is the best way to effect real change. Some believe that movements like #MeToo are not much different than so-called witch hunts aimed at destroying people and their careers without regard for due process. They argue that there are other, much more effective ways to build social justice movements than social media. Aaron Rose, a corporate diversity and inclusion consultant, says that "mainstream internet activism is a lot of calling out and blaming and shaming." According to Rose, he "used to think that those tactics created change," but he eventually realized "that I was not seeing the true change I desired. . . . We were still sad and mad. And the bad people were still bad. And everyone was still traumatized."[56]

Others disagree with this point of view. Ending a powerful person's career via online shaming is easier said than done, they argue. Very few entertainers have truly been canceled by cancel culture. Hart's career, for example, is still flourishing. Those who champion online activism say that social media platforms like Twitter, despite its many flaws, have made the world a better place. For the first time, people who are lower income and disenfranchised can finally participate in conversations that previously had excluded them. Social media has changed whose voices are being heard, they argue, and that is a good thing. As Sarah J. Jackson, a professor at the University of Pennsylvania and the coauthor of #HashtagActivism: Networks of Race and Gender Justice, writes,

> "Twitter users have disrupted a media landscape where gatekeepers . . . were for too long solely responsible for setting the agenda."[57]
>
> —Sarah J. Jackson, a professor at the University of Pennsylvania

African-Americans, survivors of gendered violence and transgender women have used Twitter to build vibrant communities and to influence news and politics. . . . Twitter users have disrupted a media landscape where gatekeepers—in an industry that has always fallen short when it comes to race and gender diversity—were for too long solely responsible for setting the agenda of what we talked about as a country.[57]

Using Social Media to Shame Corporations

People use social media to call out racism, sexism, and xenophobia, but online platforms like Facebook and Twitter have also proved to be surprisingly effective tools for shaming corporations that mistreat their customers. Although many people worry about online mobs attacking and scarring individuals, most do not fear being so careful when it comes to corporations. "Corporations don't feel," says Ohio State University law professor Doug Berman. "There are times when we do want to put the hurt on a corporation, especially if it's a corporation who hurt the community."[58]

One of the most well-known corporate shamings began at Chicago's O'Hare International Airport in April 2017, when a fully boarded, sold-out United Airlines flight was about to take off. Before the plane left the gates, an agent announced that four passengers would need to get off the plane to make room for staff members who had to fly to another location. Despite being offered money in the form of vouchers and a seat on a later flight, none of the passengers volunteered. The agent then said that four passengers would be chosen by computer. Three of the passengers chosen agreed to get off the plane, but the fourth, David Dao, a sixty-nine-year-old Vietnamese American, refused, saying he was a doctor and had to see patients. The situation escalated, airport security was called, and in the ensuing struggle, Dao was knocked unconscious before being violently dragged off the plane. He was later taken to the hospital with a concussion, a broken nose, and the loss of two front teeth.

The entire incident was filmed by passengers, who then uploaded the videos to social media. One of the videos was shared 87,000 times and viewed 6.8 million times in less than a day. United Airlines became the butt of late-night comedians' jokes, and internet memes skewering the airline also started making the rounds. There were calls to boycott the airline by social media users around the world. Even President Donald Trump weighed in on the subject, saying the airline's treatment of its customer was "horrible."[59]

To make matters worse, the CEO of United, Oscar Munoz, at first praised and defended the crew's actions while claiming the passenger was "disruptive and belligerent." The intense public outcry that followed this statement forced Munoz to change his stance, and he apologized, saying, "No one should ever be mistreated this way."[60] After Dao threatened a lawsuit, he and United Airlines reached a confidential settlement, reportedly worth millions.

The damage done to the reputation of United Airlines was considerable. Three days after the incident, a poll of nineteen hundred people showed that 79 percent of prospective fliers would rather fly on a different airline than United, and 44 percent said they would not fly United even if other airlines were more expensive and took longer to reach their destinations. The incident also prompted industry changes. Some airlines enacted new policies, such as no longer overbooking flights. Others promised that already boarded passengers would never be asked to leave their seats.

Many believe this extraordinary public shaming of United Airlines is an example of helpful or productive shaming. This is the type of shaming humanity's ancestors used as they tried to help

United Airlines became the target of public shaming following an incident in which a passenger was dragged off a flight after he refused to give up his seat on an overbooked airplane.

individuals reform their bad behavior so they could become productive members of the tribe again. Toxic shame, on the other hand, simply makes someone feel fundamentally worthless, with no hope for growth. This is the type of shame used by bullies. While it is not always easy to use shame effectively and fairly, there are benefits to getting it right. "We might share concerns about a shame-filled world that leads to individual suffering and worry that punishment online is disproportionate and lacks due process," writes Jennifer Jacquet, the author of *Is Shame Necessary? New Uses for an Old Tool*. "But shaming, aimed well, cautiously and at the right time, can improve society."[61]

Chapter Five

Preventing Online Shaming and Bullying

James was sixteen years old when he realized he was a cyberbully. He was using Ask.fm, a social network site where users ask people questions. He was just fooling around at first, sending stupid questions to people from his school. However, it quickly escalated, and James soon found himself abusing other people anonymously. "The feeling of not having to worry about people knowing who you are is powerful and addictive," he says. "I found myself resorting to abusing others when I was bored, upset, lonely or angry. It made me feel like I was important and influential in people's lives."[62]

Like James, many cyberbullies report feeling lonely and bored, and the sense of power that bullying on social media can give them becomes addictive. Even though cyberbullying can be anonymous, such as James's, it can still give them a sense that they are popular. Partly this is due to how many people can view the bullying online. Calli Tzani-Pepelasi, a psychology lecturer at the University of Huddersfield, England, says that in school, teens "may be sitting next to each other but prefer to bully each other

47

through social media, as that way their actions can be viewed by more and they feel a false sense of fame."[63]

In recent years, more experts are realizing that understanding the motivations of the cyberbully, while not excusing the behavior, is a good first step to preventing or stopping online bullying. Any kind of bullying is a learned behavior, which means that it can be unlearned. For James, his time as a cyberbully came to an end when he began to realize the true nature of the harm he was inflicting on others. "I began to read suicide stories of teenagers close to my age. . . . When I found out that they took their lives because of online trolls and cyber bullies . . . I decided enough was enough, I needed to stop."[64]

Ending the Cycle in Schools

During the 1990s and early 2000s, zero-tolerance bullying policies became popular in schools. *Zero tolerance* means that teachers and administrators cannot use their personal judgment when dealing with a bullying incident. They must impose strict punishment regardless of the circumstances or personalities involved. As a result, these policies are sometimes derided as "zero-intelligence" policies.

In many cases, zero-tolerance policies were enforced unfairly. Critics charged that they disproportionately targeted minorities, students with disabilities, or those from low-income backgrounds. In addition, the punishment usually included school suspensions, which can contribute to a student's sense of isolation and lead to feelings of hopelessness—which are associated with suicidal behavior in adolescents. However, the strongest case against zero-tolerance policies is that they do not stop bullying.

In recent years, many health experts have come to believe that it is important to look beyond the *bully* and *victim* labels. Schools need to address the needs of both victims and bullies in a more balanced way. In fact, many bullies have been the victims of bullying themselves at some point. According to a 2018 study by the *Journal of Medical Internet Research*, cyberbullies also experience depression, anxiety, and suicidal thoughts, although to a lesser extent than victims of bullying. As one teacher says, "All of these kiddos need positive reinforcement and understanding, both the kids who it's happening to, and also the ones who are bullying."[65]

A growing number of school officials have found that the most effective way to prevent bullying is to use positive reinforcement and intervention, with compassion for both sides. Teachers have found that kids who bully usually have underlying issues, such as problems at home, that contribute to the behavior. And victims of bullying often do not have the support they need to develop confidence, which can make it difficult for them to report bullying or respond to it effectively. "It has to be a community effort," says one first-grade teacher. "We teach them about bullying, but they're also learning the right ways to behave in a group situation, in a school community."[66] Research suggests that

Under zero-tolerance policies, teachers and school administrators are forced to impose strict punishments when dealing with a bullying incident.

this kind of approach results in a significant reduction in bullying while improving the social atmosphere of the school.

Adults play a major role in effective bullying prevention. For any antibullying policy to work, there needs to be at least one adult that a child can trust and confide in. For sixteen-year-old James, that person was his mother. "If you feel depressed or upset, and begin to turn to bullying, or are being bullied, I strongly advise you to talk to an adult. . . . Since my mom found out what I had been doing on the internet, she has made a special effort to ensure that I am busy and getting the most from my life."[67]

Is Cyberbullying a Crime?

In October 2019, a high school student in New Jersey was arrested and charged with online harassment. He allegedly posted comments online encouraging an elementary school girl to kill herself. He also sent her a photo of a man holding a gun to his head. The girl reported the incidents to school authorities. "I'm glad they [arrested] him,"

Some people favor arresting those who engage in cyberbullying, arguing that parents and schools are incapable of stopping the abuse.

In November 1995, President Bill Clinton and twenty-two-year-old White House intern Monica Lewinsky began an affair that would lead to Clinton's impeachment. The sensational details of their encounters became the butt of late-night jokes as Lewinsky became an international laughingstock. "Overnight, I went from being a completely private figure to a publicly humiliated one worldwide," says Lewinsky. "I was patient zero of losing a reputation on a global scale almost instantaneously. . . . When this happened to me . . . there was no name for it. Now we call it cyberbullying."

During the past few years, Lewinsky has become a high-profile advocate against cyberbullying, speaking out about her own experience of being harassed, shamed, and ridiculed. In her speeches, she asks people to support victims of online bullying and shaming. No one, she says, deserves to be treated the way she was. Making people pay a very public price for their private actions shows a profound failure of empathy. "Public shaming as a blood sport has to stop," said Lewinsky in a 2015 TED (Technology, Entertainment, Design) talk. "We need to return to a long-held value of compassion, compassion and empathy."

Quoted in Samantha Vincenty, "What Is Monica Lewinsky Doing Now? Hulu's *Hillary* Revisits the 1998 Scandal," *Oprah Magazine*, March 6, 2020. www.oprahmag.com.

Monica Lewinsky, "The Price of Shame," TED2015, March 20, 2015. www.ted.com.

one local resident said. "If you have the mentality to do this as a teenager what are you gonna do when you're an adult?"[68] But another resident called the incident "a little extreme. Kids make mistakes. It's the only way we learn in life."[69]

Every state has some form of antibullying law, but there were no specific cyberbullying laws until around 2005. Today, almost every state prohibits electronic harassment, but cyberbullying is a threat that parents, school administrators, and legislators alike are unsure of how to handle. The result is that enforcement of cyberbullying laws in the courts has varied widely.

People who support arresting and charging cyberbullies with a crime argue that cyberbullying can cause severe emotional and mental distress in victims that can lead to self-harm. Cyberbullies target their victims with malicious intent, invading their privacy and harassing them in order to cause pain and humiliation. Schools and parents, they argue, are often incapable of stopping this abuse, which means the criminal justice system must step in to punish the offenders. As New York City council member Mark Weprin says, "Your right to throw a punch ends at someone else's nose and I think your right to post an insult should end where it affects a child's mental state."[70]

People who oppose prosecuting cyberbullies argue that criminalizing online behavior can infringe on the right to free speech, which is protected by the First Amendment. Cyberbullying should be addressed by schools and parents, they contend, not the criminal justice system. And making cyberbullying a crime, they argue, will not stop kids from bullying. "Cyberbullying is a serious concern that all communities must confront," says New York Civil Liberties Union attorney Corey Stoughton. "But there are better and more constructive ways to address the problem than giving children criminal records."[71]

Social Media's Response

According to a 2018 survey by the Children's Society, a charity known for its research into the well-being of children, 83 percent of teens want social media companies to do more to prevent cyberbullying. Most of the respondents said there were too few consequences for people who engage in bad behavior online, compared to the offline world. "Social media companies should take complaints more seriously. If someone reports something, they shouldn't take days to review it, they should literally just remove it straight away,"[72] said one fifteen-year-old.

Many teens report that cyberbullying is rampant on Instagram. Over the past few years, the social media platform has introduced a number of initiatives aimed at stamping out unwanted behavior. The most important tool it uses in its fight against

While most antibullying policies encourage parents and educators to report and punish bullying, not everyone agrees. Izzy Kalman is an educator, a school psychologist, and the author of *Bullies to Buddies: How to Turn Your Enemies into Friends*. He believes that the best way to stop bullying is to treat the bully as a friend instead of an enemy and to avoid getting angry or defensive.

Kalman's method encourages young people to solve problems on their own instead of having adults act like law enforcement officers, which often escalates to more aggression. He says that punishing kids for using certain words teaches them that words are harmful. "The message given today is that although sticks and stones can break my bones, words can kill me, but that is counterproductive," Kalman explains. If someone is committing a crime against you, he says, you should go to the authorities, "but not because they're insulting you or don't want to sit with you at lunch. . . . Nobody can guarantee their children a life without difficulties. If you protect your children from the social challenges of life, it weakens them."

Quoted in Estelle Erasmus, "How to Bullyproof Your Child," *New York Times*, May 23, 2019. www.nytimes.com.

online harassment is an artificial intelligence engine called Deep-Text, which scans words for context and meaning.

Instagram already uses DeepText to detect a variety of prohibited content, such as nudity, child exploitation, and material related to terrorism. But figuring out what constitutes cyberbullying is a bigger challenge because context plays such a large role in social interactions. For example, some derogatory terms might be used as forms of endearment in certain circumstances, but the DeepText algorithms might not be able to tell the difference. Eventually, Instagram hopes DeepText will be smart enough to detect and remove cyberbullying on its own. But that day is still far off. "Our algorithms aren't yet as good as people when it comes to understanding context,"[73] says Bettina Fairman, Instagram's director of community operations.

Another problem faced by social media companies is that teenage behavior and language both change and evolve over time. This means that a platform's definition of bullying can

Instagram has acted to stamp out cyberbullying, which many teens say is rampant on that social media platform.

become outdated. To counter this, Instagram uses focus groups of teens and parents to get feedback about the types of cyberbullying they have encountered on the platform. For example, some teens feel bullied when their exes post photos showing off their new boyfriends or girlfriends in order to rub in the fact that they have someone new. As a result, Instagram trained its algorithm to detect this kind of bullying, which it calls a "betrayal."

Despite Instagram's efforts, cyberbullying is still a major problem on the platform. The size of the platform and the complex and ever-changing nature of online harassment will make it difficult to completely get rid of the problem. But executives at the company believe the tools they are building will continue to improve and allow users to have more control over their online experience. "It's odd to realize that what Instagram is describing—a planetary-scale A.I. [artificial intelligence] surveillance system for detecting and classifying various forms of teenage drama—is both technically possible and, sadly, maybe necessary," writes Kevin Roose, who studies the intersection of technology, business, and culture. "It should make us all question whether a single company should have so much power over our social relationships, or whether any platform of Instagram's size can be effectively governed at all."[74]

A Crisis in Empathy

Many experts believe that one of the best ways to prevent online shaming and bullying is to teach people how to be more empathetic. Empathy is the ability to feel what another person is feeling. Empathy is different than sympathy, which is feeling *for* someone through shared emotions. Empathy, instead, is feeling *with* someone by imagining how that person feels.

Unfortunately, research has shown an alarming decrease in empathy levels. A major study at the University of Michigan tracked empathy levels in college students and found a 40 percent decline over the past three decades; meanwhile, levels of narcissism increased by 58 percent. The decline in empathy was particularly steep from 2000 on. "Our children became very plugged in around the year 2000," says Michele Borba, an educational psychologist and parenting expert. "It's very hard to be empathetic and feel for another human being if you can't read another person's emotions. You don't learn emotional literacy facing a screen. You don't learn emotional literacy with emojis."[75]

> "You don't learn emotional literacy facing a screen. You don't learn emotional literacy with emojis."[75]
>
> —Michele Borba, an educational psychologist and parenting expert

People empathize most easily when they can see the suffering of others with their own eyes. But the rise of the internet and social media has dramatically reduced the amount of time spent talking to people face-to-face. Activities that used to bring people together, such as joining bowling leagues or civic organizations, have been replaced by spending more time online—and alone.

The decline of reading is also linked to the decline of empathy. One study reveals that the more preschoolers read, the better their ability to understand the emotions of others. Another study shows that adults who read more fiction are more empathic. Unfortunately, leisure reading in the United States is at an all-time low, according to a 2018 survey from the Bureau of Labor Statistics. And research conducted in 2020 shows that children today read less frequently than any previous generation.

The good news is that the sharp decline in empathy has revealed that empathy is more fluid than previously thought. If empathy levels can change, it means they can also go up. Humanity is not necessarily doomed to become a society of lonely, self-obsessed individuals. "It's tempting to blame technology for its ill effects, and many people have. But it is only a tool, and it reshapes human interactions based on what we design and how we use it," says Jamil Zaki, a Stanford University neuroscientist and the author of *The War for Kindness: Building Empathy in a Fractured World*. "The Internet is also an unprecedented empathic opportunity—to deeply see the lives of people around the world, on their own terms, and be seen in return. The way technology affects us in the years to come is up to us."[76]

Introduction: A New Form of an Old Problem

1. Quoted in Emily S. Rueb, "A Teenager Killed Himself After Being Outed as Bisexual. His Family Wants Justice," *New York Times*, September 30, 2019. www.nytimes.com.
2. Quoted in Allyson Chiu, "A Teen's Intimate Messages to Another Boy Were Leaked by Classmates. Hours Later, He Killed Himself, His Family Says," *Washington Post*, September 30, 2019. www.washingtonpost.com.
3. Quoted in Chiu, "A Teen's Intimate Messages to Another Boy Were Leaked by Classmates."
4. Quoted in Mark Molloy, "Online Shaming: The Dangerous Rise of the Internet Pitchfork Mob," *The Telegraph* (London), June 25, 2018. www.telegraph.co.uk.
5. Quoted in Chiu, "A Teen's Intimate Messages to Another Boy Were Leaked by Classmates."

Chapter One: The Rise of Cyberbullying

6. National Crime Prevention Council, "Cyberbullying—What Is It?" www.ncpc.org.
7. Quoted in Misha Valencia, "How to Safeguard Children Against Cyberbullying," *New York Times*, September 5, 2019. www.nytimes.com.
8. Quoted in Taylor Lorenz, "Teens Are Being Bullied 'Constantly' on Instagram," *The Atlantic*, October 10, 2018. www.theatlantic.com.
9. Quoted in Valencia, "How to Safeguard Children Against Cyberbullying."
10. Quoted in Ditch the Label, "The Annual Bullying Survey 2019." www.ditchthelabel.org.
11. Quoted in *New York Times*, "Parents Often Unaware of Cyber-Bullying," October 3, 2008. www.nytimes.com.
12. Quoted in Marwa Eltagouri, "A 10-Year-Old's Schoolyard Fight Was Posted on Social Media. She Hanged Herself Two Weeks Later," *Washington Post*, December 1, 2017. www.washingtonpost.com.
13. Quoted in Lorenz, "Teens Are Being Bullied 'Constantly' on Instagram."
14. Quoted in Lorenz, "Teens Are Being Bullied 'Constantly' on Instagram."

15. Quoted in Kevin Roose, "Instagram Is Trying to Curb Bullying. First, It Needs to Define Bullying," *New York Times*, May 9, 2019. www.nytimes .com.

Chapter Two: Using Social Media to Publicly Shame

16. Quoted in Kyle Nazario, "Twitter Overwhelmingly Abhors *Esquire* Cover Story Focusing on White, Middle-Class 'American Boy,'" *Atlanta Journal-Constitution*, February 12, 2019. www.ajc.com.
17. Quoted in Nazario, "Twitter Overwhelmingly Abhors *Esquire* Cover Story Focusing on White, Middle-Class 'American Boy.'"
18. Patrick A. Coleman, "The Controversy over *Esquire*'s White 'American Boy' Cover Story Is Just . . . Sad," Fatherly, February 12, 2019. www .fatherly.com.
19. Margaret Rouse, "Internet Shaming (Online Shaming)," WhatIs.com. https://whatis.techtarget.com.
20. Robyn Kanner, "*Esquire*'s Cover Boy and Our Culture of Shame," *New York Times*, February 16, 2019. www.nytimes.com.
21. Quoted in Peter Stearns, "Does American Culture Shame Too Much—or Not Enough?," Salon, November 12, 2017. www.salon.com.
22. Quoted in Todd Leopold, "The Price of Public Shaming in the Internet Age," CNN, April 16, 2015. www.cnn.com.
23. Quoted in Jon Ronson, "How One Stupid Tweet Blew Up Justine Sacco's Life," *New York Times*, February 12, 2015. www.nytimes.com.
24. Quoted in Ronson, "How One Stupid Tweet Blew Up Justine Sacco's Life."
25. Quoted in Ronson, "How One Stupid Tweet Blew Up Justine Sacco's Life."
26. Quoted in Ronson, "How One Stupid Tweet Blew Up Justine Sacco's Life."
27. Quoted in Leopold, "The Price of Public Shaming in the Internet Age."
28. Sam Biddle, "Justine Sacco Is Good at Her Job, and How I Came to Peace with Her," *Gawker* (blog), December 20, 2014. www.gawker.com.
29. Guillaume Chaslot, "The Toxic Potential of YouTube's Feedback Loop," *Wired*, July 13, 2019. www.wired.com.
30. Quoted in Chaslot, "The Toxic Potential of YouTube's Feedback Loop."
31. Quoted in Peter Suciu, "More Americans Are Getting Their News from Social Media," *Forbes*, October 11, 2019. www.forbes.com.
32. Quoted in Nazario, "Twitter Overwhelmingly Abhors *Esquire* Cover Story Focusing on White, Middle-Class 'American Boy.'"
33. Quoted in Nazario, "Twitter Overwhelmingly Abhors *Esquire* Cover Story Focusing on White, Middle-Class 'American Boy.'"

Chapter Three: The Trauma of Being Bullied or Publicly Shamed

34. Caitlin White, "Public Shaming," Medium, December 11, 2017. www .medium.com.

35. Quoted in White, "Public Shaming."

36. Nathan Jurgenson, "Digital Dualism Versus Augmented Reality," *Nathan Jurgenson: A Social Theory and Culture Blog*, February 24, 2011. https://nathanjurgenson.wordpress.com.

37. Quoted in Ross Rosenberg, "Unearthing & Ridding Yourself of Toxic Shame," PsychCentral, July 8, 2018. www.psychcentral.com.

38. Quoted in Julie Deardorff, "Shame Returns as Punishment," *Chicago Tribune*, April 12, 2000. www.chicagotribune.com.

39. Quoted in Chris Elkins, "Bullying and Substance Abuse: Who It Affects and Why," DrugRehab.com, March 2, 2020. www.drugrehab.com.

40. Quoted in Ditch the Label, "The Annual Bullying Survey 2018." www.ditchthelabel.org.

41. Quoted in Nicole Makris, "For Kids, Bullying by Peers Is Worse than Abuse from Adults," Healthline, April 28, 2015. www.healthline.com.

42. Quoted in Jane E. Brody, "The Crisis in Youth Suicide," *New York Times*, December 2, 2019. www.nytimes.com.

43. Quoted in Brody, "The Crisis in Youth Suicide."

44. Quoted in Associated Press, "Rise in Teen Suicide Connected to Social Media Popularity: Study," *New York Post*, November 14, 2017. www.nypost.com.

45. Quoted in Joe Pinsker, "What's to Be Done About Kids and Their Phones?," *The Atlantic*, November 2, 2018. www.theatlantic.com.

46. Quoted in Eric Spitznagel, "The Internet Never Forgets," *Popular Mechanics*, November 1, 2019. www.popularmechanics.com.

47. Quoted in Ronson, "How One Stupid Tweet Blew Up Justine Sacco's Life."

48. Quoted in Spitznagel, "The Internet Never Forgets."

Chapter Four: Calling Out Bad Behavior

49. Quoted in David Moye, "Angry White Dude's Rant About People Speaking Spanish in NYC Goes Viral," Huffington Post, May 16, 2018. www.huffpost.com.

50. Laila Lalami, "The Social Shaming of Racists Is Working," *The Nation*, May 24, 2018. www.thenation.com.

51. Quoted in Joseph Burgo, "Why Shame Is Good," Vox, April 18, 2018. www.vox.com.

52. Eric Posner, "A Terrible Shame," Slate, April 9, 2015. www.slate.com.

53. Mark Joseph Stern, "No, Aaron Schlossberg Will Not Be Disbarred over His Racist Rant," Slate, May 18, 2018. www.slate.com.

54. Michael Arceneaux, "Kevin Hart Is Not the Victim of His Own Controversy," *Esquire*, December 10, 2018. www.esquire.com.

55. Quoted in Anna North, "#MeToo's Latest Critics Say They Want to Help the Movement. Why Are They Shaming Women?," Vox, August 27, 2019. www.vox.com.

56. Quoted in Aja Romano, "Why We Can't Stop Fighting About Cancel Culture," Vox, December 30, 2019. www.vox.com.

57. Sarah J. Jackson, "Twitter Made Us Better," *New York Times*, December 27, 2019. www.nytimes.com.
58. Quoted in Tovia Smith, "Companies 'Named and Shamed' for Bad Behavior," *Weekend Edition Sunday*, National Public Radio, March 7, 2010. www.npr.com.
59. Quoted in Lisa Marie Segarra, "President Trump Says the United Airlines Incident Was 'Horrible,'" *Fortune*, April 12, 2017. www.fortune.com.
60. Quoted in Erin McCann, "United's Apologies: A Timeline," *New York Times*, April 14, 2017. www.nytimes.com.
61. Jennifer Jacquet, "Public Shaming Makes the World a Better Place," *Wired*, July 24, 2015. www.wired.com.

Chapter Five: Preventing Online Shaming and Bullying

62. Quoted in Elizabeth Soal, "Confessions of a Cyberbully," Netdoctor, February 3, 2014. www.netdoctor.co.uk.
63. Quoted in Kelly Oakes, "Why Children Become Bullies at School," BBC Future, September 15, 2019. www.bbc.com.
64. Quoted in Soal, "Confessions of a Cyberbully."
65. Quoted in Molly Pennington, "Zero Tolerance Bullying Policies Aren't Working: Here's a Better Solution," Noodle, November 20, 2014. www.noodle.com.
66. Quoted in Pennington, "Zero Tolerance Bullying Policies Aren't Working."
67. Quoted in Soal, "Confessions of a Cyberbully."
68. Quoted in Infobase, "Cyberbullying: Should Cyberbullies Be Prosecuted?," December 3, 2019. http://icof.infobaselearning.com.
69. Quoted in Infobase, "Cyberbullying."
70. Quoted in Aaron Short, "Cyberbullies Get First Amendment Protection," *New York Post*, July 1, 2014. www.nypost.com.
71. Quoted in Short, "Cyberbullies Get First Amendment Protection."
72. Quoted in BBC News, "Social Media Firms 'Failing' to Tackle Cyber-Bullying," February 26, 2018. www.bbc.com.
73. Quoted in Roose, "Instagram Is Trying to Curb Bullying."
74. Roose, "Instagram Is Trying to Curb Bullying."
75. Quoted in Alon Shwartz, "Our Kids Are Losing Their Empathy & Technology Has a Lot to Do with It," Medium, September 20, 2017. www.medium.com.
76. Quoted in Emma Seppälä, "Empathy Is on the Decline in This Country. A New Book Describes What We Can Do to Bring It Back," *Washington Post*, June 11, 2019. www.washingtonpost.com.

American Association of Suicidology (AAS)

www.suicidology.org

Founded in 1968 by Edwin S. Shneidman, the AAS promotes research, public awareness programs, public education, and training for professionals and volunteers. In addition, the AAS serves as a national clearinghouse for information on suicide. Its mission is to promote the understanding and prevention of suicide and support those who have been affected by it.

Cybersmile Foundation—www.cybersmile.org

The Cybersmile Foundation is an award-winning nonprofit organization committed to digital well-being and tackling all forms of abuse and bullying online. It works to promote kindness, diversity, and inclusion by building a safer, more positive digital community.

Ditch the Label—https://us.ditchthelabel.org

One of the largest antibullying nonprofit organizations in the world, Ditch the Label provides digital online support programs through its website and partnerships with online games and social networks. Its mission is to combat bullying by tackling the root issues and to support young people ages twelve through twenty-five who are impacted.

End to Cyber Bullying (ETCB)—www.endcyberbullying.org

The ETCB is a nonprofit organization founded by Samuel Lam and David Zhao in 2011 in the hopes of creating a social networking world devoid of cyberbullying. The ETCB hopes to help teens, parents, educators, and others to identify, prevent, and ultimately stop cyberbullying.

STOMP Out Bullying—www.stompoutbullying.org

The leading national antibullying and cyberbullying organization for kids and teens in the United States, STOMP Out Bullying works to reduce and prevent bullying, cyberbullying, and other digital abuse. It teaches effective solutions for responding to all forms of bullying as well as educating kids and teens in school and online.

StopBullying.gov—www.stopbullying.gov

A federal government website managed by the US Department of Health and Human Services, StopBullying.gov provides information from various government agencies on what bullying is, what cyberbullying is, who is at risk, and how best to prevent and respond to bullying.

Books

Michele Borba, *UnSelfie: Why Empathetic Kids Succeed in Our All-About-Me World*. New York: Touchstone, 2016.

J.A. Hitchcock, *Cyberbulling and the Wild, Wild Web*. London: Rowman & Littlefield, 2016.

Justin W. Patchin, *Bullying Today: Bullet Points and Best Practices*. Thousand Oaks, CA: Sage, 2017.

Sue Scheff, *Shame Nation: The Global Epidemic of Online Hate*. Naperville, IL: Sourcebooks, 2017.

Jean M. Twenge, *iGen: Why Today's Super-Connected Kids Are Growing Up Less Rebellious, More Tolerant, Less Happy—and Completely Unprepared for Adulthood—and What That Means for the Rest of Us*. New York: Atria, 2017.

Jamil Zaki, *The War for Kindness: Building Empathy in a Fractured World*. New York: Crown, 2019.

Internet Sources

Michael Nuccitelli, "42 Examples of Cyberbullying & Cyberbullying Tactics," iPredator. www.ipredator.co.

David Rosen, "Crime and Public Shaming," CounterPunch, April 15, 2016. www.counterpunch.org.

Loretta Ross, "I'm a Black Feminist. I Think Call-Out Culture Is Toxic," *New York Times*, August 17, 2019. www.nytimes.com.

Anya Skrba, "Cyberbullying Statistics, Facts, and Trends (2020)," First Site Guide, October 28, 2019. https://firstsiteguide.com.